SONGS OF THE 60's

THE DECADE SERIES

D1400126

HAL•LEONARD®
CORPORATION
7777 W. BLUEMOUND RD. P.O. BOX 13819 MILWAUKEE, WI 53213

The Sixties

by Stanley Green

"All the News
That's Fit to Print"

The New York Times.

7 A.M. EXTRA

VOL. CX ... No. 37,545   NEW YORK, WEDNESDAY, NOVEMBER 9, 1960   FIVE CENTS

KENNEDY IS APPARENT VICTOR; LEAD CUT IN TWO KEY STATES; DEMOCRATS RETAIN CONGRESS

John F. Kennedy

"Let the word go forth from this time and place, to friend and foe alike, that the torch has been passed to a new generation of Americans — born in this century, tempered by war, disciplined by a hard and bitter peace, proud of our ancient heritage — and unwilling to witness or permit the slow undoing of those human rights to which this nation has always been committed, and to which we are committed today at home and around the world."

Those bold, eloquent words of the nation's 35th President, John F. Kennedy, rang out from the Capitol steps on a raw January 20, 1961. But far from inaugurating an era of unity, idealism and action, they would, ironically, usher in the most divisive decade of the 20th Century. For the Sixties were years of turbulence and conflict as the American people suffered through three traumatic assassinations, the ongoing struggle for civil rights, and the deepening involvement in the war in Vietnam.

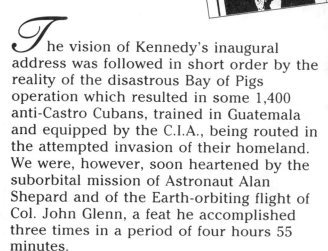

The motorcade in Dallas after President Kennedy had been shot

The vision of Kennedy's inaugural address was followed in short order by the reality of the disastrous Bay of Pigs operation which resulted in some 1,400 anti-Castro Cubans, trained in Guatemala and equipped by the C.I.A., being routed in the attempted invasion of their homeland. We were, however, soon heartened by the suborbital mission of Astronaut Alan Shepard and of the Earth-orbiting flight of Col. John Glenn, a feat he accomplished three times in a period of four hours 55 minutes.

Kennedy's firm resolve helped end the Soviet missile crisis in Cuba, but this was to be his last major achievement. On November 22, 1963, while riding in a motorcade in Dallas, he was assassinated by Lee Harvey Oswald who, two days later, was gunned down by a local nightclub owner.

A march on the 1st Anniversary of Rev. Martin Luther King's death

The death of Kennedy and his succession by Vice President Lyndon Johnson came amidst the growing, often violent confrontations resulting from the efforts of Rev. Martin Luther King and his followers to protest the policy of racial segregation then being enforced in the South. Among the events of the Sixties that marked the struggle: the admission of James Meredith as the first black student at the University of Mississippi; the murder of civil-rights leader Medgar Evans; the killing of three white activists — Goodman, Schwerner and Cheney — in Philadelphia, Mississippi; the mammoth rally in Washington where 250,000 heard King's stirring "I have a dream" speech; the bombing that cost the lives of four black girls in a Birmingham church; the adoption of the Civil Rights Act barring discrimination in public accommodations; the arrest of Dr. King and 2,600 demonstrators in Selma, Alabama; the riots in the nation's ghettos during the long hot summers from 1964 through 1967; and the assassination of Dr. King the following year that fanned the flames of more violence and looting. Then, as the country seemed to be reeling from one tragic event to another, Sen. Robert Kennedy was shot to death in a Los Angeles hotel.

Demonstrators both for and against the Vietnam War.

Overseas, the United States was finding itself mired deeper and deeper in the rice paddies of Vietnam. At the beginning of the decade, there were 1,000 military advisers, a figure that rose to 543,400 combat troops before a phased withdrawal was begun in 1969. During the war — the longest in U.S. history — the country was rent by continued anti-war demonstrations, including student protests on college campuses and the disruption of the 1968 Democratic National Convention in Chicago. Beset by Communist troops of North Vietnam and guerrilla units of the Vietcong in the South, the American forces were ill-equipped to wage jungle warfare and the many bombings of the North were unable to force the Communist leader, Ho Chi Minh, to the conference table. Following the Tet offensive and the My Lai massacre, however, the United States ordered a unilateral cease-fire of the bombings and Hanoi finally agreed to peace talks. By the end of the Sixties — with the war still on — American combat deaths had risen to almost 34,000.

Other areas of the world were also exploding with strife. In the former Belgian Congo, the newly established Republic of the Congo underwent severe birth pains when Premier Patrice Lumumba was murdered and Katanga Province leader Moise Tshombe tried to establish an independent nation. In the Dominican Republic, Dictator Rafael Trujillo was shot to death. In Ghana, Premier Kwami Nkruma was ousted in a coup and the military junta that took over was soon crushed by another coup. In Indonesia, tens of thousands were massacred in a government crackdown to foil a Communist takeover. In South Africa, Prime Minister Verwoerd was stabbed to death. In the Middle East, the Six-Day War between Israel and it's neighbors, Egypt, Jordan, Syria, and Iraq, ended with the Jewish state occupying territory four times its own size. In Czechoslovakia, the liberal policies of Premier Alexander Dubcek were brutally halted by the invasion of Soviet Union and Warsaw Pact troops. And in Libya, a fanatic army captain, Muammar al-Qadaffi, put an end to the reign of King Idris.

The Sixties also saw such vivid events as the shooting down of Gary Francis Power's U-2 spy plane over Russia, the erection of the Berlin Wall, the power blackout of the northeastern states in November 1965 (and the resultant increase in the birth rate nine months later), the year-long internment of the U.S. Navy ship Pueblo by the North Korean government, and the Chappaquiddick tragedy involving Sen. Edward Kennedy. In addition, the decade gave us such diverse heroes as heavyweight champ Muhammed Ali (formerly Cassius Clay), heart-transplant pioneer Christiaan Barnard, sailboat skipper Francis Chichester, whose solo voyage around the world on the Gypsy Moth IV took 226 days, and Astronaut Neil Armstrong, the first man to set foot on the moon. Lest we forget, the era also provided a number of visual innovations and pleasures, including pop art, mini skirts, and the phenomenon known as Twiggy.

Lyndon B. Johnson

The Beatles

Anthony Newley in
"Stop The World — I Want To Get Off"

The tunes — as well as the times — were a-changin' in the Sixties. Rock and roll was declared dead only to be reborn with the arrival of the mop-headed foursome known as The Beatles (from Liverpool, no less). The folk music craze twanged in and out. Songs preaching social justice and expressing anti-war sentiments brought adherents to Bob Dylan and Joan Baez. Big bands showed no signs of a comeback, except for those with the near-symphonic sounds of Mantovani and Henry Mancini. And glitzy discothèques became the rage, introducing such dancefloor gyrations as the twist, the frug, the mashed potato, the Watusi, and the monkey.

Perhaps the most noticeable influence was the British invasion led by The Beatles ("I Want to Hold Your Hand," "She Loves You"). In their wake came Marian Faithfull ("As Tears Go By"), Petula Clark ("Downtown"), Gerry and the Pacemakers ("Ferry Cross the Mersey"), Tom Jones ("It's Not Unusual"), and The Seekers ("Georgy Girl"). Even that traditional American form, the musical theatre, made way for the arrival of such British writers as Lionel Bart with *Oliver!* (featuring "As Long as He Needs Me") , and Anthony Newley and Leslie Bricusse with two shows, *Stop the World — I Want to Get Off* ("What Kind of Fool Am I?") and *The Roar of the Greasepaint — The Smell of the Crowd* ("Who Can I Turn To?").

Those Were The Days

Words and Music by GENE RASKIN
Sung by MARY HOPKIN on Apple Records

TRO The Richmond Organization   95¢

$\mathcal{E}$ngland wasn't the only foreign country to supply songs for the U.S. pop market during the decade. A German folk song, "Muss I Denn Zum Stadtele Haus," was turned into "Wooden Heart," one of Elvis Presley's successes, and a Russian folk song provided the source for Mary Hopkin's hit, "Those Were the Days." The Danish singer Bent Fabric (né Bent Fabricus Bjerre) brought over his "Alley Cat" (né "Omkring et Flygel"), the Belgian Singing Nun Soeur Sourire achieved fame with her own "Dominique," Roy Clark scored impressively with "Yesterday When I Was Young," the English version of the French "Hier encore," and French composer-conductor André Popp's "L'Amour est bleu" became — not too surprisingly — "Love Is Blue," a hit single for Claudine Longet. The bossa nova beat proliferated for a while thanks to the appeal of Astrud Gilberto's recording of the Brazilian "Girl from Ipanema," written by Antonio Carlos Jobim, and Frank Sinatra returned auspiciously to the top of the charts with "Strangers in the Night" ("Zoobee zoobee zoo"), indited by German orchestra leader Bert Kaempfert. Also winning favor were songs emanating from foreign films, notably "More," the theme of the Italian documentary *Mondo Cane,* and Michel Legrand's "Watch What Happens," adapted from the love duet in the French *Umbrellas of Cherbourg.*

Barbra Streisand in "Funny Girl"

sung in *The Fantasticks,* which — at this writing — has been running Off Broadway for over 26 years!); "Sunrise, Sunset," a wistful rumination about the passing of time that was introduced in *Fiddler on the Roof;* the philosophical "People," sung by Barbra Streisand in *Funny Girl;* "Cabaret," an insinuating invitation first proffered in the show of the same name; and "My Cup Runneth Over," an expression of love that served as a duet for Mary Martin and Robert Preston in *I Do! I Do!* Also in the canorous vein were two romantic standards, "Fly Me to the Moon" and "I Left My Heart in San Francisco," both benefiting from Tony Bennett's distinctive interpretations.

A number of songwriters of the Sixties gave voice to their feelings about contemporary issues. In the forefront was Pete Seeger, whose output included such pieces as "If I Had a Hammer," a rollicking proclamation of brotherhood "all over this land"; "Turn! Turn! Turn!," a call for peace based on the Bible's "Book of Ecclesiastes"; and "Where Have All the Flowers Gone?," a somber reflection on the lives lost in battle. In addition, there was "One Tin Soldier," an ironic, allegorical message about the futility of war, and "San Francisco (Be Sure to Wear Some Flowers in Your Hair)," a paean to the lifestyle of hippies and flower children.

*V*ery much a part of the spirit of the Sixties were the vocal and instrumental groups that appealed primarily — but not exclusively — to teenagers. These went by such fanciful rubrics as Ruby and the Romantics ("Our Day Will Come"), The Dixie Cups ("Chapel of Love"), Little Anthony and the Imperials ("Goin' Out of My Head"), The Mamas and the Papas ("California Dreamin'," "Monday, Monday"), Booker T. and the MG's ("Groovin'"), The McCoys ("Hang on Sloopy"), The Turtles ("Happy Together"), Steam ("Na Na Hey Hey, Kiss Him Goodbye"), and The Fifth Dimension ("Up, Up and Away").

*T*here were, of course, the more traditional, melodic songs, mostly from Broadway musicals, that continued to catch the public fancy. Among them: "Try to Remember," a haunting ballad still being

"The Fantasticks"

*Robert Preston
and Mary Martin
in "I Do! I Do!"*

Woodstock   AP Photo

*P*robably never before this decade had music played such an important part in the lives of young people. Deeply affected by the tumult and turmoil all around them, their anti-establishment attitude was marked by long hair and slovenly dress, strong opposition to war, and their advocacy of civil rights, sexual freedom, and drugs. As something of a symbol of the age, some 300,000 converged on the town of Bethel, New York, for a three-day marathon rock concert known as Woodstock. They may not have been exactly what President Kennedy had in mind in his inaugural address, but they were unquestionably a new generation of Americans.

ALLEY CAT SONG

Words by JACK HARLEN
Music by FRANK BJORN

Moderately slow

He goes on the prowl each night like an Al - ley Cat,

Look - in' for some new de - light like an Al - ley Cat.

She can't trust him out of sight, there's no doubt of that.
He don't know what "faith - ful" means, there's no doubt of that.

AS TEARS GO BY

Words and Music by MICK JAGGER,
KEITH RICHARD and ANDREW LOOG OLDHAM

AS LONG AS HE NEEDS ME
(From the Columbia Pictures - Romulus film "OLIVER!")

Words and Music by LIONEL BART

BY THE TIME I GET TO PHOENIX

Words and Music by Jimmy Webb

CABARET
(From the Musical "CABARET")

Music by JOHN KANDER
Words by FRED EBB

CALIFORNIA DREAMIN'

Words and Music by JOHN PHILLIPS

CAN'T HELP FALLING IN LOVE

Words and Music by
GEORGE WEISS, HUGO PERETTI &
LUIGI CREATORE

Moderately Slow

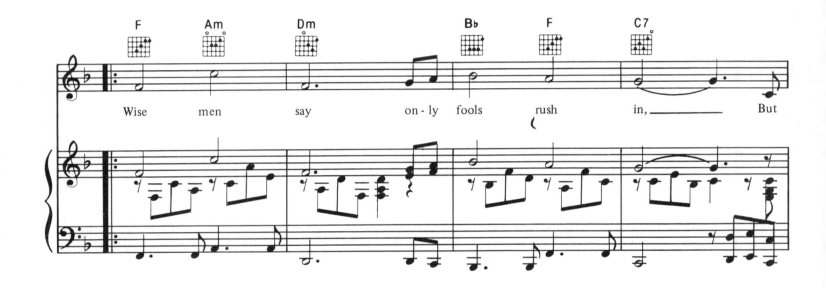

Wise men say on-ly fools rush in, _____ But

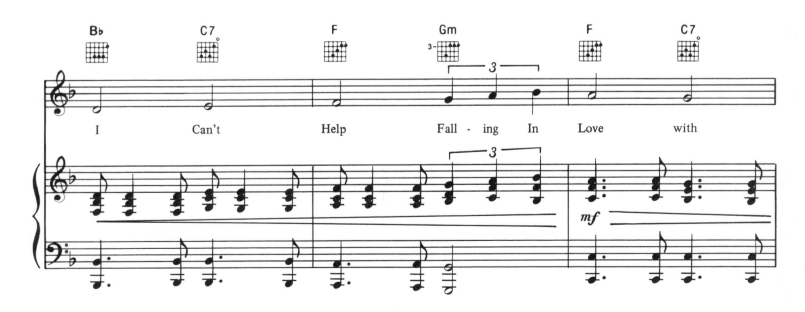

I Can't Help Fall-ing In Love with

DAYDREAM

Words and Music by JOHN SEBASTIAN

3. *Whistle*
Whistle
Whistle
Whistle
And you can be sure that if you're feelin' right,
A daydream will last till long into the night.
Tomorrow at breakfast you may pick up your ears,
Or you may be daydreamin' for a thousand years.

CHAPEL OF LOVE

Words and Music by
PHIL SPECTOR, ELLIE GREENWICH
and JEFF BARRY

* Repeat from * to * for fade-out ending

DOMINIQUE

By SOEUR SOURIRE, O.P.
English lyrics by NOEL REGNEY

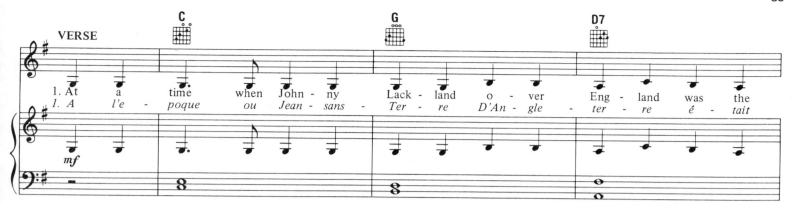

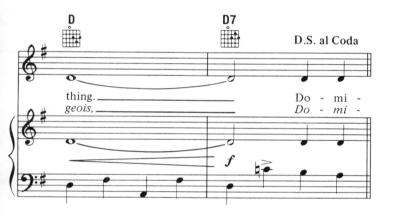

ENGLISH	FRENCH
2. Now a herectic, one day, Among the thorns forced him to crawl. Dominique with just one prayer, Made him hear the good Lord call. (To Chorus)	2. Certain jour un hérétique Par des ronces le conduit Mais notre Père Dominique Par sa joie le convertit. (Au refrain)
3. Without horse or fancy wagon, He crossed Europe up and down. Poverty was his companion, As he walked from town to town. (To Chorus)	3. Ni chameau, ni diligence Il parcourt l'Europe à pied. Scandinavie ou Provence Dans la sainte pauvreté. (Au refrain)
4. To bring back the straying liars And the lost sheep to the fold, He brought forth the Preaching Friars, Heaven's soldiers, brave and bold. (To Chorus)	4. Enflamma de toute école Filles et garçons pleins d'ardeur, Et pour semer la Parole Inventa les Frères-Prêcheurs. (Au refrain)
5. One day, in the budding Order, There was nothing left to eat. Suddenly two angels walked in With a load of bread and meat. (To Chorus)	5. Chez Dominique et ses frères Le pain s'en vint à manquer Et deux anges se présentèrent Portant de grands pains dorés. (Au refrain)
6. Dominique once, in his slumber, Saw the Virgin's coat unfurled Over Friars without number Preaching all around the world. (To Chorus)	6. Dominique vit en rêve Les prêcheurs du monde entier Sous le manteau de la Vierge En grand nombre rassemblés. (Au refrain)
7. Grant us now, oh Dominique, The grace of love and simple mirth, That we all may help to quicken Godly life and truth on earth. (To Chorus)	7. Dominique, mon bon Père, Garde-nous simples et gais Pour annoncer à nos frères – La Vie et la Vérité. (Au refrain)

DOWNTOWN

Words and Music by TONY HATCH

Medium Rock

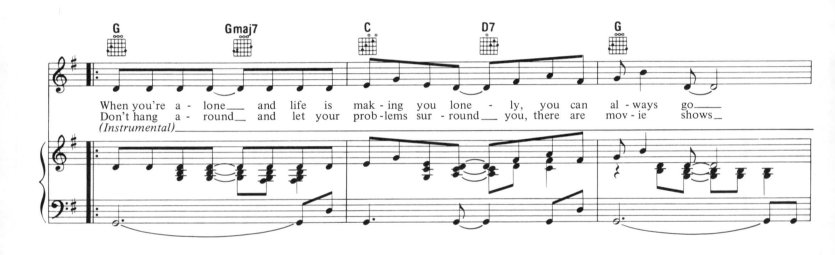

When you're a-lone___ and life is mak-ing you lone-ly, you can al-ways go___
Don't hang a-round___ and let your prob-lems sur-round___ you, there are mov-ie shows___
(Instrumental)___

down-town.   When you've got wor-ries, all the noise and the hur-ry seems to
down-town.   May-be you know___ some lit-tle plac-es to go___ to where they

MCA MUSIC

GEORGY GIRL

Words by JIM DALE
Music by TOM SPRINGFIELD

THE EXODUS SONG

Words by PAT BOONE
Music by ERNEST GOLD

FERRY CROSS THE MERSEY

Words and Music by GERRARD MARSDEN

FLY ME TO THE MOON
(In Other Words)

Words and Music by
BART HOWARD

THE GIRL FROM IPANEMA
(Garôta De Ipanema)

Original Words by VINICIUS DE MORAES
English Words by NORMAN GIMBEL
Music by ANTONIO CARLOS JOBIM

MCA MUSIC

GOIN' OUT OF MY HEAD

Words and Music by TEDDY RANDAZZO
and BOBBY WEINSTEIN

GREEN GREEN GRASS OF HOME

Words and Music by CURLY PUTMAN

Moderately Slow

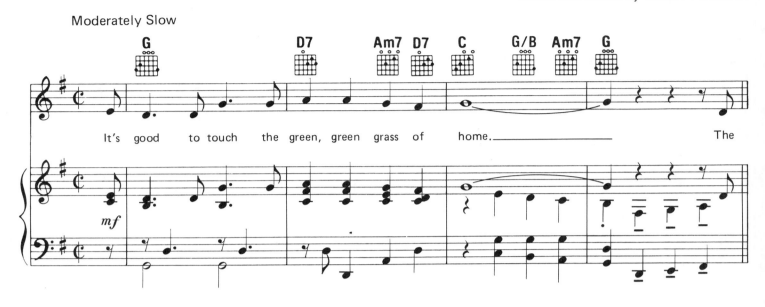

It's good to touch the green, green grass of home._____ The

old home town___ looks the same as I step down from the
(Spoken:) Then I awake and look around me at four gray

old home house is still stand-ing tho' the paint is cracked and
walls

train,___ and there to meet me is my ma-ma___ and
dry,___ and there's that old oak tree that I used to
that surround me and I realize that I was only dreaming.

55

HONEY

Words and Music by
BOBBY RUSSELL

Moderately

See the tree how big it's grown, but friend, it has-n't been too long it was-n't big. I
She was al-ways young at heart, kind-a dumb and kind-a smart and I loved her so.

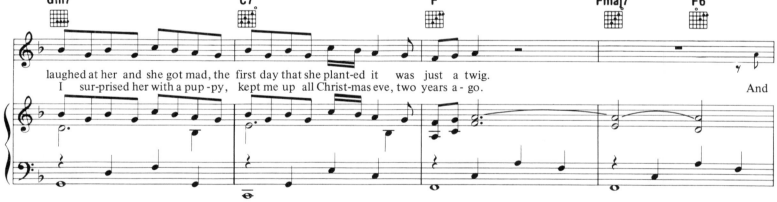

laughed at her and she got mad, the first day that she plant-ed it was just a twig. And
I sur-prised her with a pup-py, kept me up all Christ-mas eve, two years a-go.

Then the first snow came and she ran out to brush the snow a-way so it would-n't die, Came
it would sure em-bar-rass her when I came home from work-ing late 'cause I would know That

GROOVIN'

Words and Music by FELIX CAVALIERE
and EDWARD BRIGATI, JR.

HANG ON SLOOPY

Words and Music by
BURT RUSSELL and VICK KNIGHT

HAPPY TOGETHER

Words and Music by GARRY BONNER
and ALAN GORDON

HELLO MARY LOU
(GOODBYE HEART)

Words and Music by GENE PITNEY
and C. MANGIARACINA

Moderately

I LEFT MY HEART IN SAN FRANCISCO

Words by DOUGLASS CROSS
Music by GEORGE CORY

I WANT TO HOLD YOUR HAND

Words and Music by JOHN LENNON
and PAUL McCARTNEY

IF I HAD A HAMMER
(THE HAMMER SONG)

Words and Music by LEE HAYS
& PETE SEEGER

LITTLE GREEN APPLES

Words and Music by
BOBBY RUSSELL

IF I WERE A CARPENTER

Words and Music by TIM HARDIN

IT'S MY PARTY

Words and Music by HERB WIENER,
WALLY GOLD and JOHN GLUCK, JR.

Moderately bright

No-bod-y knows____ where my John-ny has gone,____ But
Play all my rec - ords, keep danc-ing all night,____ But
Ju-dy and John - ny just walked thru the door,____

Ju-dy left____ the same time.
leave me a-lone____ for a-while,
Like a queen____ with her king,

Why was he
'Til John-ny's
Oh, what a

IT'S NOT UNUSUAL

Words and Music by GORDON MILLS
and LES REED

MCA MUSIC PUBLISHING

mad with an-y-one.____ It's not un-u-su-al____ to be

sad with an-y-one.____ But if I ev-er find that you've changed____

____ at an-y-time,____ It's not un-u-su-al____ to

find that I'm____ in love____ with you._____

KING OF THE ROAD

Moderately, with a bounce

Words and Music by ROGER MILLER

Trail-er for sale or rent, rooms to let fif-ty cents.
Third box-car mid-night train, des-ti-na-tion: Ban-gor, Maine.

No phone, no pool, no pets; I ain't got no cig-a-rettes. Ah, but
Old worn-out suit and shoes; I don't pay no un-ion dues. I smoke

two hours of push-ing broom buys a eight by twelve four bit room. I'm a
old sto-gies I have found, short but not too big a-round. I'm a

LOVE IS BLUE
(L'AMOUR EST BLEU)

English Lyric by BRIAN BLACKBURN
Original French Lyric by PIERRE COUR
Music by ANDRÉ POPP

Moderately Slow (with an easy flow)

MONDAY, MONDAY

Words and Music by JOHN PHILLIPS

Moderately

1,3. Mon - day, Mon - day, so good to me
2. Mon - day, Mon - day, Can't trust that day

Mon - day morn - in', it was all I hoped it would be.
Mon - day, Mon - day, some - times it just turns out that way.

Oh, Mon - day morn - in', Mon - day morn - in' could-n't guar - an - tee
Oh, Mon - day morn - in', you give me no warn - in' of what was to be

MORE
(Theme From MONDO CANE)

English Words by NORMAN NEWELL
Music by R. ORTOLANI and N. OLIVIERO

Moderately

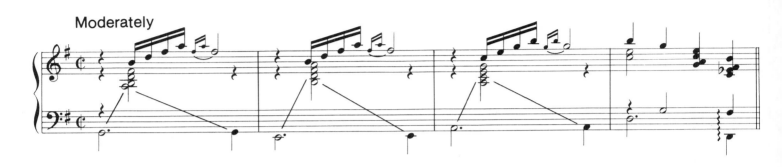

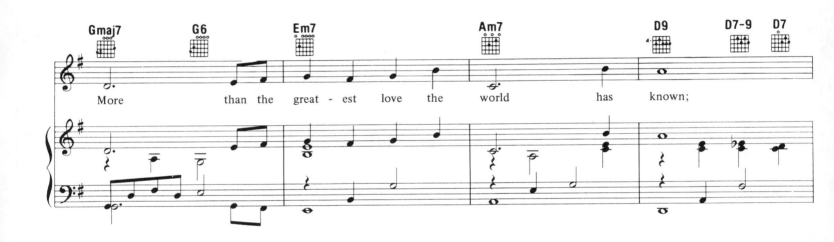

More than the great-est love the world has known;

This is the love I'll give to you a-lone.

ONE TIN SOLDIER

Words and Music by DENNIS LAMBERT
and BRIAN POTTER

Moderately slow rock tempo

Lis - ten child - ren to a sto - ry that was writ - ten long a - go___
So the peo - ple of the val - ley sent a mes - sage up the hill___
Now the val - ley cried with an - ger mount your hors - es, draw your sword___

'bout a king - dom on a moun - tain and the val - ley folk be - low.
ask - ing for___ the___ bur - ied trea - sure tons of gold___ for which they'd___ kill.
and they killed___ the___ moun - tain peo - ple so they won___ their just re - ward.

MY COLORING BOOK

Words and Music by
FRED EBB and
JOHN KANDER

Freely

For those who fan-cy co-lor-ing books, and lots of peo-ple do, ___

Slow 4, in tempo

Here's a new one for you. ___

These ___ are the eyes that watched her as she walked a - way,

(She walked a -

MY CUP RUNNETH OVER

(From "I DO! I DO!")

Words by TOM JONES
Music by HARVEY SCHMIDT

Some- times in the morn- ing when shad- ows are
times in the ev- 'ning when you do not

deep, I lie here be- side you, just watch- ing you
see, I stud- y the small things just you do con- stant-

Na Na Hey Hey Kiss Him Goodbye

Words and Music by
GARY DeCARLO, PAUL LEKA,
and DALE FRASHUER

OUR DAY WILL COME

Words by BOB HILLIARD
Music by MORT GARSON

PAPER ROSES

Words by JANICE TORRE
Music by FRED SPIELMAN

PEOPLE
(From "FUNNY GIRL")

Words by BOB MERRILL
Music by JULE STYNE

PLEASE, PLEASE ME

Words and Music by JOHN LENNON
and PAUL McCARTNEY

Last night I said these words to my_____ girl
You don't need me to show the way_____ love

I know you nev-er e-ven try_____ girl
Why do I al-ways have to say_____ love

Come on, come on, come on, come on, Please please me oh

SHE LOVES YOU

Words and Music by JOHN LENNON
and PAUL McCARTNEY

Moderately, with a beat

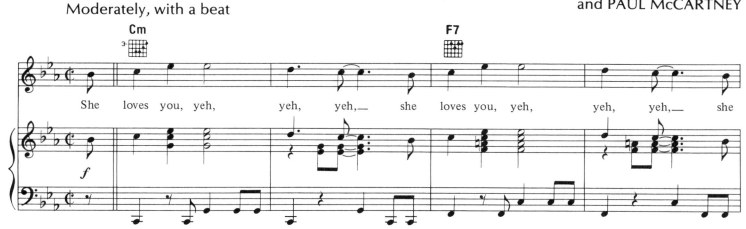

She loves you, yeh, yeh, yeh,— she loves you, yeh, yeh, yeh,— she

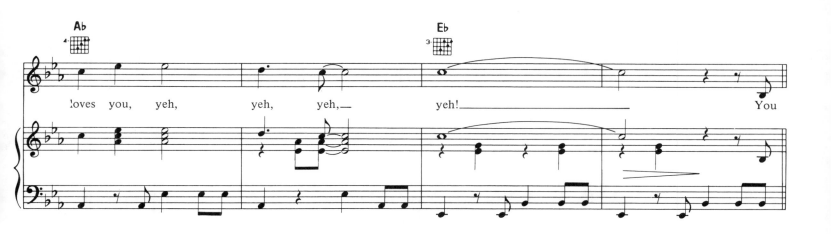

loves you, yeh, yeh, yeh,— yeh!_____ You

think you've lost your love,____ Well, I saw her yes - ter - day-yi-yay. It's
said you hurt her so,____ She al - most lost her mind, And
know it's up to you,____ I think it's on - ly fair,____

122

SAN FRANCISCO
(BE SURE TO WEAR SOME FLOWERS IN YOUR HAIR)

Words and Music by JOHN PHILLIPS

SPANISH HARLEM

Words and Music by
JERRY LEIBER and PHIL SPECTOR

There is a rose in Span-ish Har-lem,

A red rose up in Span-ish Har-lem, It is a
With eyes as

spec-ial one___ It's nev-er seen the sun.___ It on-ly comes out when the moon is on the
black as coal___ that look down in my soul, And start a fire___ there and then I lose con-

STRANGERS IN THE NIGHT

Words by CHARLES SINGLETON
and EDDIE SNYDER
Music by BERT KAEMPFERT

MCA MUSIC PUBLISHING

Sunrise, Sunset
(From the Musical "FIDDLER ON THE ROOF")

Words by SHELDON HARNICK
Music by JERRY BOCK

THAT'S LIFE

Words and Music by DEAN KAY
and KELLY GORDON

THINGS

Words and Music by
BOBBY DARIN

Think-in' 'bout the things we used to do ____

do. ____ I still can hear the juke-box soft-ly

play - ing ____ (play - ing) ___ And the face I see each day be-longs to

you. (be-longs to you.) ___ Though there's not a sin-gle sound and there's no -

THOSE WERE THE DAYS

Words & Music by GENE RASKIN

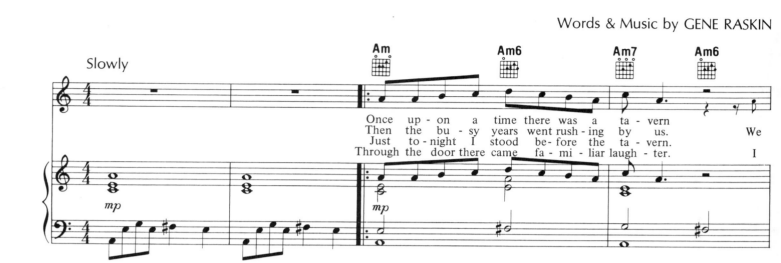

TRY TO REMEMBER
(From "THE FANTASTICKS")

Words by TOM JONES
Music by HARVEY SCHMIDT

TURN! TURN! TURN!
(To Everything There Is A Season)

Words from the Book of Ecclesiastes
Adaption and Music by PETE SEEGER

151

THE TWIST

Words and Music by HANK BALLARD

UP, UP AND AWAY

Words and Music by JIM WEBB

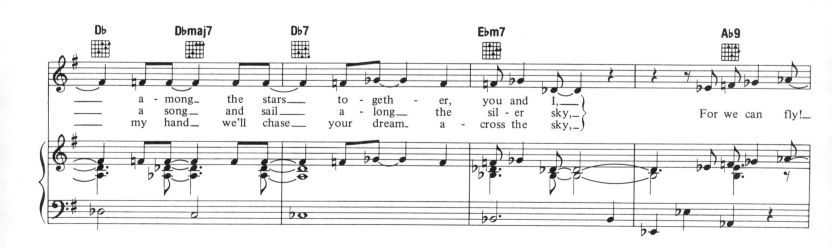

WATCH WHAT HAPPENS

English Words by NORMAN GIMBEL
Music by MICHEL LEGRAND

WHAT KIND OF FOOL AM I?

(From the Musical Production "STOP THE WORLD - I WANT TO GET OFF")

Words and Music by
LESLIE BRICUSSE
and ANTHONY NEWLEY

WHERE HAVE ALL THE FLOWERS GONE?

Words & Music by PETE SEEGER

3. Where have all the young men gone? Long time passing.
Where have all the young men gone? Long time ago.
Where have all the young men gone?
They're all in uniform.
Oh, when will they ever learn?
Oh, when will they ever learn?

4. Where have all the soldiers gone? Long time passing.
Where have all the soldiers gone? Long time ago.
Where have all the soldiers gone?
They've gone to graveyards, every one.
Oh, when will they ever learn?
Oh, when will they ever learn?

5. Where have all the graveyards gone? Long time passing.
Where have all the graveyards gone? Long time ago.
Where have all the graveyards gone?
They're covered with flowers, every one.
Oh, when will they ever learn?
Oh, when will they ever learn?

6. Where Have All The Flowers Gone? Long time passing.
Where Have All The Flowers Gone? Long time ago.
Where Have All The Flowers Gone?
Young girls picked them, every one.
Oh, when will they ever learn?
Oh, when will they ever learn?

A WHITER SHADE OF PALE

Words and Music by KEITH REID
and GARY BROOKER

WHO CAN I TURN TO
(When Nobody Needs Me)

(From the Musical Production "THE ROAR OF THE GREASEPAINT - THE SMELL OF THE CROWD")

Words and Music by LESLIE BRICUSSE
and ANTHONY NEWLEY

Slowly with expression

WOODEN HEART

Words and Music by
FRED WISE, BEN WEISMAN,
KAY TWOMEY and BERTHOLD KAEMPFERT

Moderately

Can't you see I love you, Please don't break my heart in

two, That's not hard to do, 'Cause I don't have a

YESTERDAY, WHEN I WAS YOUNG
(Hier Encore)

English Lyric by HERBERT KRETZMER
Original French Text and Music by
CHARLES AZNAVOUR

Moderately